Monumental Follies
of the
Isle of Wight

Ian Williams

Rockpool Publications

Monumental Follies of the Isle of Wight by Ian Williams

First Published in 2008 by
Rockpool Publications
Aprils View, Alverstone Road, Queens Bower,
Sandown, Isle of Wight PO36 0NY
© Ian Williams 2008
ISBN 978-0-9558376-0-9

Ian Williams has asserted his right to be identified
as the author of this work.
Printed by Crossprint
Newport, Isle of Wight

Book design by Stephen Darlington

CONTENTS

INTRODUCTION

WHAT IS A FOLLY?

There is an element of the whimsical, the capricious and the fanciful about folly expressed in the definition in the Readers Digest Universal Dictionary; "an ornamental building or structure built purely for decoration." Lord Berner, talking of Faringdon Tower, said, "The great point of this tower is that it will be entirely useless." In this sense a folly is a building which has no purpose except to be there.

In the seventeenth and eighteenth centuries, it was the fashion for the sons of the wealthy families to tour Europe as part of their education. 'The Grand Tour' was often preferred to a frequently ruinous university education. Whilst travelling in Italy and Greece, these young and wealthy Englishmen marvelled at the splendid temples and palaces they saw that expressed the power and grandeur of the classical world. On their return they sought to recreate these splendours in their own country seats, transforming their ancestral homes with ideas borrowed from classical architecture.

Men like Lancelot 'Capability' Brown were employed to lay out the grounds and build temples, grottos, gateways and pavilions in the

Classical style as ornaments. The 'eyecatchers' at Appuldurcombe and Swainston built to enhance the view enter this category. The turretted towers at Appley and Luccombe, though watchtowers and viewpoints were really just quaint decorations.

The Readers Digest Universal Dictionary gives a second definition of a folly as "a costly undertaking having an absurd or ruinous outcome." Similarly, the Oxford English Dictionary defines a folly as "any costly structure considered to have shown folly in the builder."

Some of the entries in this book have a full measure of foolishness. A lighthouse built on a hill prone to fog, Spindler's vain attempt to build a harbour that nearly left him bankrupt, Palmerston's forts that so rapidly became white elephants and the non-revolving cone at St Mary's Hospital all fall into this second category.

To add further to the confusion of definitions, some say a folly is 'a structure that is not what it appears' or a 'misunderstood' building. If a building is a curiosity and makes you stop, and scratch your head, and ask yourself "Why?" then consider it a folly. Miss Bull's Folly and Thomas Lett's rotunda were memorials but nonetheless fanciful creations and curiosities. The Folly Inn is included because it is the Folly Inn!

CHAPTER ONE

WORSLEY WONDERS

Cook's Castle, the Worsley obelisk and the follies at
Sea Cottage

For nearly three hundred years the Worsleys had been the island's premier family with their seat in the "valley of apples" at Appuldurcombe House. It was the last Worsley to live at Appuldurcombe, the third Sir Richard who was responsible for the follies at Appuldurcombe and St Lawrence, but perhaps his greatest folly was his decision to marry Seymour Dorothy Fleming, the 17 year old daughter of Sir John Fleming, "for love," said Gibbon, "and £80,000." Despite her dowry she was to prove an incorrigible flirt, unfaithful wife and far more trouble than she was worth.

Seymour had a string of affairs with Appuldurcombe's aristocratic guests which threatened to turn Sir Richard into a laughing stock and tarnish the image of the island's first family. Lady Worsley's affair with the Earl of Peterborough was chronicled by Horace Walpole and Sir Richard was lampooned in The Memoirs of Sir Finical Whimsy and his Lady. In 1782 Sir Richard sued Captain George Bisset of Knighton for "criminal conversation" with his wife. The trial, presided over by Lord Mansfield, was a sensation and the printed text of the proceedings became a bestseller.

The crucial evidence centred around a bizarre incident in the Public Baths at Maidstone. A rapt and silent court heard that Sir Richard "had absolutely raised the defendant upon his shoulders to view his naked wife while bathing, and at the same time called to her, saying 'Seymour! Seymour! Bisset is looking at you.'" Though Sir Richard won his case he failed to win the £20,000 damages he sought. Instead the court awarded him just one shilling on the grounds that he had "been privy to the prostitution of his wife." This unhappy and very public affair was the ruin of his career and Sir Richard relinquished his Court positions and left the country for a tour of the East.

The Worsleys originally came from near Manchester and took their name from the village of Worsley in the heart of industrial Lancashire. James Worsley was a page at the court of Henry VII and 'whipping boy' to the young prince who, on becoming King Henry VIII, rewarded James with a knighthood and a monopoly of official posts in the Isle of Wight, including those of sheriff, coroner and military captain. On the island James met and married Anne Leigh. On the death of her father, Sir John Leigh, James took possession of the Appuldurcombe estate and became the richest man on the island.

It was Sir Robert Worsley who demolished the Elizabethan house, boasting that "I have not left one stone standing," and set about building the present Palladian mansion in the early 1700's. By 1712 lack of money put a stop to the work and it was left unfinished. Sir Robert died in 1747 and it was left to the third and last Sir Richard Worsley, who succeeded to the estate in 1768, to complete it.

At various times Sir Richard was MP for Newport and Newtown, Governor of the Isle of Wight and Colonel of the South Hampshire Militia. He became Clerk of the Green Cloth, Comptroller of George III's Household and a Privy Councillor. In his later years he was appointed Plenipotentiary to the Doges of Venice.

Those who knew Sir Richard paint a picture of a man hard to like. By all accounts he condoned many of his wife's affairs and had a reputation as a bit of a 'rake.' Sir Richard went on the Grand Tour with the historian Edward Gibbon's friend D'Eyverdun as tutor, returning in 1772. Gibbon wrote of Worsley "I see many alterations, and little improvement. From an honest wild English buck, he is grown a

Appuldurcombe House and the Worsley Obelisk

Philosopher . . . He speaks in short sentences, quotes Montaigne, seldom smiles, never laughs, drinks only water, professes to command his passions, and intends to marry in five months." The political philosopher Jeremy Bentham, who met Sir Richard in Constantinople in 1786, found him "haughty, selfish and mean."

It was in the 1770's that Sir Richard engaged Lancelot 'Capability' Brown to design the landscape of the grounds of Appuldurcombe. The house sits in a valley surrounded by downland which forms a natural ampitheatre and among the planned features were two "eyecatchers" on either side of the valley. The first was an obelisk 70 feet high made of Cornish granite and designed to 'stop the eye.' It was built by Sir Richard in 1774 on Appuldurcombe Down as a memorial to Sir Robert Worsley. In 1831 it was struck by lightning and reduced to its present height.

On the opposite side of the valley, just below St Martin's Down, was Cook's Castle which Sir Richard describes in his History of the Isle of Wight as "the ruin of an ancient castle, which serves as a point of view from the house." It is unclear whether this "eyecatcher" was adapted from an existing ruin or was built by Sir Richard as a mock gothic sham to enhance his view.

Gilpin, on his tour of the island, remarked that the "continuous horizontal ridge might hurt the eye, if it were not crowned with a castle. This object seems well executed, and is certainly well placed." Jenkinson's *Practical Guide to the Isle of Wight* of 1879 refers to it as "nothing more than a modern turreted tower" embowered with trees. G. Harvey Betts, who wrote *Shanklin as a Health Resort*, thought it "of questionable taste."

When Sir Richard died in 1805 the estate passed to his neice who married Charles Pelham, later the first Earl of Yarborough. He was a great yachtsman and became the first Commodore of the Royal Yacht Squadron. He has his own monument on top of Culver Down. Two small cannon were brought to Cook's Castle from the Earl of Yarborough's yacht, presumably to make it look more like a castle! It became a favourite place for picnicers and in the mid nineteenth century was occupied by W. Fulford who served refreshments in the surrounding gardens. Jenkinson's Guide tells us that visitors were permitted to climb the tower for the view and that the person who lived at the castle, "for a small remuneration," would supply hot water to picnicers. Today, all that remains is a small stone plinth to mark the site.

Sir Richard was an art lover and he set off in 1785 on a tour of the Mediterranean, the Near East, the Levant and Russia. He brought back with him the most important collection of Greek marbles yet seen in England, plus antique gems and other works of art. Later, whilst Minister in Venice in 1797 he bought a magnificent collection of paintings from an Italian nobility down on its luck and fearful of Napoleon. He also bought up paintings dispersed by the French Revolution.

He turned Appuldurcombe House into a museum and his exhibits were catalogued, annotated and illustrated in the 2-volume Museum Worsleianum. According to Thomas Pennant there were "marbles in almost all the rooms below stairs . . . over the door leading to the eating room is a beautiful and precious fragment of marble found at Athens, representing Jupiter and Minerva receiving vows and supplications from an Athenian family. In the same room is an interesting monument found in the Athenian acropolis in 1785."

Cook's Castle

Sir Richard owned much of St Lawrence and rather than live in a museum he moved into 'Sea Cottage,' built in 1794 at Steephill on the Undercliff. It is not surprising, in view of Sir Richard's taste for Greco-Roman marbles, that he should decorate the gardens of the cottage, which stretched to the cliff, with three classical 'temples.' There was a pavilion designed from the Temple of Minerva at Athens; on the cliff there was a little temple, called the Seat of Virgil, with a bust of the poet; and a Grecian style greenhouse based on the Temple of Apollo at Corinth. This last building, which survives in the grounds of Lisle Combe, was used to house fifteen orange and lemon trees in the winter. George Brannon's 1827 engraving of Sea Cottage, then Lord Yarborough's Marine Villa, shows the greenhouse.

When George III presented him with six bronze cannon taken from a captured French privateer, Sir Richard built a miniature fort for his battery of guns on the edge of the cliff overlooking a small bay. The cannon were said to have been cast from the melted bells of Nantes Cathedral. The bay, now Sir Richard's Cove, was called Battery Bay and the guns could still be seen as late as 1939 but where they are now nobody knows. The battery served no purpose other than ornamental and so may with justification be considered another of Sir Richard's follies.

Sea Cottage showing the greenhouse

Sir Richard was certainly foolhardy in attempting to cultivate vines so close to the sea. In 1793 he planted two and a half acres of land at St Lawrence with seven thousand White Muscadine and Plante Verde vines and engaged a Breton, Jean Julian, to tend the vineyard. But despite a favourable climate the salt spray proved too much, the wine scant in quantity and poor in quality. Three years after Sir Richard's death the ground was returned to lawns.

Battery Bay

CHAPTER TWO

THE SHAKESPEARE MONUMENT

Lett's celebration of the famous bard

Mention the name Letts and one automatically thinks of diaries. In 1796 John Letts, a bookbinder by trade, established a stationery business in the arcades of London's Royal Exchange. The merchants and traders who bought stationery items from this shop needed a means of recording the movements of stock and controlling their finances. John Letts responded in 1812 by creating the world's first Commercial Diary called 'Lett's diary or bills owed book and almanack.'

The diary quickly became established as an essential feature of commercial life. He introduced detailed information sections and by the 1820's he was publishing the first modern style diary ranges. When Thomas Letts took over the business from his father he decided to concentrate on diaries. By 1839 he was offering twenty eight varieties to the public including foolscap folios and pocket versions. So successful was the business that he built large factories at New Cross and widened the range to include calendars, ledgers, clerical, medical and other specialised diaries. Thackeray, author of *Vanity Fair*, endorsed Lett's diaries when he made them the text of a New Year sermon published in *Cornhill Magazine*.

Professor Letts, a lecturer at Oxford, bought South View House along the old Undercliff Road between Niton and Blackgang. The house was built in the Italianate style with a small turret and a garden enclosed by circular terrace walks. Immediately behind towered the upper cliff. No doubt it was acquired as a retreat from the bustle of his London business, a place where he could sit in peace and enjoy his beloved Shakespeare.

In 1864, to mark the tercentenary of the birth of Shakespeare, Letts erected, on a nearby knoll, a small rotunda of a Doric temple containing a statuette of the poet and playwright. Ward Lock's *Pictorial and Descriptive Guide of 1910* likens it to the Burns Memorials; inscribed on it were these lines from *The Tempest*:-

> "He sits, 'mongst men like a descended god;
> He hath a kind of honour sets him off,
> More than mortal seeming."

The choice of quotation reveals the adoration Letts felt for the bard and the small yet grand monument is more like a shrine than memorial, a place of adulation and worship.

Beneath it, set in the ivy covered stone wall that flanked the old road, was a spring of crystal water. But the water no longer flows from the battered stone scallop; nor can you read the fragmented inscription that surrounds the flow pipe. It is taken from *Two Gentlemen of Verona*, Act II, Scene IV:- "The water nectar, and the rocks pure gold." Set beside a road once busy with walkers and carriages, it was a temptation to the weary traveller to stop and an invitation to reflect upon the genius of the greatest of England's poets.

Today the house is abandoned, victim of the landslides which have carried away the road on either side, leaving it to await its inevitable fate in spookish silence. The grounds are overgrown though the stone steps through the terraces can be traced. It is still accessible from Blackgang along paths made by those who still dare to live here in the tumbled landscape and who come and go like wraiths. However, the council have erected signs prohibiting entry on safety grounds.

The spring is easy to miss hidden beneath its ivy mantle; opposite a set of steps past a makeshift home and tended garden on a terrace. No trace remains of the rotunda, perhaps removed to safety somewhere, taken away as a trophy or garden ornament. But there is a carte de visite, fore-runner of the postcard, published by Fletcher Moor of Ventnor which shows the monument to be an elegant, classical memorial.

The Fountain & Shakespeare Memorial, Blackgang, Isle of Wight.

CHAPTER THREE

THE THIMBLE CAIRN

Miss Bull's Folly on Limerstone Down

Northcourt Manor in the village of Shorwell lies tucked away in a secluded valley surrounded by tall trees. Shortly after the Dissolution it came into the possession of the Leighs and it was Sir John Leigh who built the present house in 1615. This large Jacobean mansion caught the eye of Richard Bull, the heir to Watchingwell near Newport, on a visit he made to the island in 1783 with his wife and daughters. Twelve years later he bought it from the Leigh's heir.

Bull came from Ongar in Essex, the son of a turkey merchant. He stood for Parliament in 1756 and was returned unopposed as the MP for Newport. He remained in the seat until 1780 receiving as a sinecure the secret service pension worth £600 a year. Despite his role as MP he was a totally apolitical figure and there is no record of him having ever spoken in the House.

Bull was a cultured man with a passion for books, paintings and good cuisine. He was a friend of the writer and wit Horace Walpole and both were avid art collectors. Bull was a renowned "head hunter," a collector of engraved portraits and he amassed a large collection considered to be of national importance. Bull indulged his passion in friendly rivalry with Walpole. In 1806, *Gentleman's Magazine* wrote, in their obituary of Bull, "He early evinced an enthusiasm for the arts, particularly that of engraving, which with much study, he cultivated into a refined knowledge almost exclusively his own."

As for books Richard Bull had a not inconsiderable library of three thousand volumes and the kitchens concocted delicacies and the cellars provided wines for his visitors. Count Waldstein was to write, following one such visit:-

> "... How the cellars of North Court, the Kitchen, the rooms
> Were all waiting for me, with the housemaids and grooms;
> How the books and the cooks with a Rhyme or a Jelly
> Were to stock *uti decet* my wisdom and belly . . .

Westward from Northcourt run two parallel ridges, the northern one higher, which come together at Limerstone Down. Where they meet there is a small knoll, a vantage point overlooking the farmland below and along to the sea. Here, according to a local tale, a sailor's lover kept a lonely vigil awaiting his return from a three year voyage. She watched the sea for his ship, and while she watched she sewed for her wedding trousseau. He never came back but she carried on sewing and watching till she died.

One of Bull's daughters, Elizabeth, loved this melancholy story with its theme of suffering for love. Perhaps she imagined herself the unrequited lover striding along the narrow ridge, her hair flowing in the breeze. Or perhaps the lover was really Elizabeth's younger sister Catherine, who died young, perhaps of a broken heart? At any rate, Elizabeth was sufficiently moved to have a stone monument erected on the knoll.

Some sources refer to this as a small tower and indeed some of the old maps have identified it as Coombe Tower because the land on which it stood belonged to Coombe Farm, Brighstone. Others call it the Thimble Cairn in reference to the story but it became universally known as Miss Bull's Folly. It was dismantled during the second world war for fear that it could be used as a navigation mark by enemy aircraft and the stones were used to make hard standing in

Miss Bull's folly at Limerstone Down

a Brighstone farmyard. The field in which the tower stood is still
known today as Monument Ground.

Sir Richard and Elizabeth shared an enthusiasm for landscape
gardening and terraced much of the grounds and built some structures
which may also be considered follies. Elizabeth inspired the mausoleum
to her sister Catherine which is described by Davenport Adams in his
Isle of Wight History, Topography and Antiquities of 1882:- "In a
woody hollow, formerly a chalk pit, and overhung by a large ash tree,
is a low stone building like a Gothic chapel, with a thatched roof and
painted windows containing a stately sarcophagus of white marble on
the front of which are carved in bas relief a male and female figure
hanging over an urn." On a tablet beneath the urn were inscribed some
mawkish lines written by her father.

On another tablet detached from the monument was another
inscription, equally sentimental and full of vapid religious faith. It
calls upon the spirit of the place to:-

> Restore that calm Religion only gives,
> Correct those thoughts desponding Grief conceives:

On the other side of the road to Northcourt on a hillock known as
Mount Ararat she had a 'Temple of the Sun' erected. According to
Barber this was "never more than a rustic summerhouse, crowning
a very steep ascent and . . . commanding a very wide and delightful
prospect." No trace of this remains. There was also an 'alpine bridge'
across the road a replica of which still spans the main road today.

Whatever the truth behind the story, Elizabeth cuts a lonely figure and missed the companionship of her sister. As her father wrote:-

> She was their comfort, joy and pride -
> With her their every pleasure died

Elizabeth never married. So did the sorrowful tale strike a chord in her lonely heart sufficiently strong to move her to build the sad memorial?

CHAPTER FOUR

FOOLISH FORTS

Lord Palmerston's Follies

During his second term as Prime Minister, from 1859 – 65, Lord Palmerston was accused of building needless defences at great cost against an imaginary enemy. Supporters claimed he took wise precautions in unsettled times to ensure Britain's security. So did Palmerston panic or did he show remarkable prudence? Were Palmerston's forts follies?

The review of Britain's coastal defences undertaken by a Royal Commission which Palmerston instigated was motivated by two factors. Firstly, an inflated fear of Britain's traditional enemy, France, especially after Bonaparte's nephew, Louis Napoleon, seized power in a coup d'etat and assumed the title of Emperor. Secondly, the rapid advances in modern technology were forcing a revolution in naval warfare. Britain was forced to compete with France in the application of modern science to warfare in order to keep ahead.

Britain was suspicious of France believing that revenge for Waterloo was a long term objective. French actions were taken to confirm this. There was the completion of the naval base at Cherbourg, directly opposite Portsmouth. "It is against England alone that it is constructed," wrote the *Times* on 13 July 1858. "Any blow that may be launched from Cherbourg will . . . be short, it will be straight, deadly and decisive, aimed at England's very heart." The construction of the Suez Canal would, said Palmerston, set "a French colony in the heart of Egypt" and threaten British India. He assumed it was a French plot. Napoleon's acquisition of Nice and Savoy was also seen as evidence of anti-British designs.

Palmerston believed "we have on the other side of the channel a people who, say what they may, hate us as a nation from the bottom of their hearts, and would make any sacrifice to inflict a deep humiliation upon England . . . At the head of this nation we see an able, active, wary, counsel-keeping, but ever-planning sovereign."

The transformation of the navy saw steam replace sail power and iron hulled ships replace wooden and it was the French who launched the first steam driven ironclad warship – *La Gloire* in 1859. That same year a Report on naval strength revealed that the French navy, though numerically still inferior overall, was the equal of the British navy in home waters because British ships were scattered across the globe in defence of Empire.

At the same time the development of long range rifled cannon and the substitution of explosive shells for shot threatened to make our coast defences obsolete. William Armstrong produced a breech loading cannon which nearly doubled the range of heavy guns. This created fears that the dockyards and arsenals could be bombarded from areas where no defence works currently existed.

All these factors combined to create an atmosphere of panic over French intentions and the adequacy of British defences. Palmerston's solution was threefold. There was support for the volunteer movement to try and increase the numbers available for home defence. Palmerston supplied rifles to them (and Tennyson a poem – *Riflemen, form!*) Secondly, there was to be a programme of naval construction. Lastly, a Royal Commission was appointed in August 1859 to review all of Britain's coastal defences.

The Report of the Royal Commission on the Defences of the United Kingdom favoured a series of sea forts to protect the Spithead anchorage and Portsmouth dockyard from bombardment. Support for this was drawn from the experience of the Crimean War. The barrier and the great sea forts at Kronstadt had prevented the British from attacking the naval base. The failure of the bombardment of the forts at Sebastapol was further evidence to support sea forts.

There was much opposition to the Spithead forts and the "ships versus forts" debate delayed building for two years. Some argued for a strong naval presence in the channel as a deterrent which meant more ships. Others, like Captain Coles, argued for armoured floating batteries instead of sea forts and the fight between the two ironclads, the *Merrimac* and the *Monitor*, in the American Civil War seemed to support him.

Another critic of the forts, Bernal Osborne, quoted a couplet of Gibbons that referred to the use of convicts in building the older fortifications at Portsmouth:-

"To raise this fortress of enormous Price
The head of Folly used the hand of Vice"

Osborne declared that though no vice was in question, it was certainly folly to spend millions on such forts. And so they were branded Palmerston's Follies.

Four sea forts were completed – Spit Bank, Horse Sand, No Man's Land and, later, St Helens fort at a cost, without armament, of £1,177,800. They were armed and re-armed with changes in technology but were never called upon to fulfil the task they were built for.

The sea forts weren't the only follies for which Palmerston was responsible. There were coastal batteries to defend the Needles passage, to protect the sea forts and to secure Sandown's beaches against invasion. These were supported by three new forts – Golden

Hill fort at Freshwater, Sandown granite fort and Bembridge fort on Culver Down.

Fort Victoria and Fort Albert can also be considered as follies though Palmerston was not to blame. They were built in the wake of the invasion scare of 1851/2 and were criticised by James Fergusson, Scottish architectural writer, who favoured earthworks rather than masonry forts. The advances in armament, especially the introduction of explosive shells, made both forts white elephants by the 1870s and they were taken out of front-line service and used as barracks.

CHAPTER FIVE

SPINDLER'S FOLLY

In the footsteps of Canute

Theodore Julius William Spindler was born in Berlin on April 2nd 1838 and first visited Ventnor in 1873 at the age of 35. He came for the improvement of his health and was enchanted by the beauty of the Undercliff and benefited from its mild climate. In 1881 he bought 160 acres of the Old Park estate and started to spend his fortune on projects he considered beneficial to the community.

He was an extraordinary man. He was an industrialist and millionaire who made his fortune in the manufacture of dyes. But he was no ascetic capitalist in the Victorian mould but a Radical with socialist leanings, more like his countryman Freidrich Engels. He could perhaps be best described as a Good Samaritan. He was a generous employer, introducing the short hours system on his estate, and paying his labourers the highest wages, no less than 18 shillings a week.

It was to Spindler's generosity that the inhabitants of Whitwell and Niton owe their abundant and good supply of fresh water. He spent £500 on a new peal of bells and clock at Whitwell Church. He supported Ventnor shopkeepers by not placing his large orders with London firms.

Subscriptions for the promotion of public institutions and amusements benefited from his donations.

A flavour of his opinions may be gathered from this letter to the editor of the *Ventnor Gazette* on the subject of Sunday trading: "You object to Sunday bands on piers and in parks: I want to have them. You are for closing the public-houses on a Sunday; I am for opening a good many other places besides churches and chapels. You object to the Town collecting money at the Pier when enlivened by music; I fail to see why parsons alone should have the monopoly to make money on a Sunday. You want to drive the people into your churches and chapels; I do not in the least object to their going there, if they like. But I object to your Sabbatarian robbing the poor man who has to work during

Habour wall at Binnel bay

the six days of the week of the seventh part of his life, otherwise hard enough; and just of that only part which could be made enjoyable."

Spindler was always forthright and outspoken in his views and was a regular contributor to the letters pages of the *Ventnor Gazette* and *The Gnat*. He wrote a pamphlet of 130 pages, entitled *A Few Remarks about the Isle of Wight, Bournemouth etc* in which he rued the lack of foresight of Ventnor's inhabitants in not providing more amenities for visitors. Spindler contended that if the people of Ventnor continued to bury their heads in the sand, a "new town" called Undercliff would spring up, a sort of St Lawrence-on-Sea and that his estate at Old Park "presented a magnificent field for the enterprise of a capitalist."

So in 1886 Spindler began to throw his money into an ambitious project to build a sea wall to Ventnor as the starting point for this new town. He built stone groynes and the sea wall went up at Binnel Bay but it wasn't long before he was foiled in his attempt to hold back the sea, just like King Canute. While work was going on he was the largest employer in the area. But he died before his work was finished, on December 3rd 1889, aged 51, and, as the *County Press* remarked "the mind that was so ready to plan and the hand that was so prompt to execute are gone." The remains of his wall can still be seen at Binnel Bay, known as Spindler's Folly.

CHAPTER SIX
SANDROCK CHALYBEATE SPRING

Or what Waterworth's water was worth

In the eighteenth century medical knowledge was still primitive and there was a general belief in the medicinal properties of chalybeate spring waters rich in iron salts. Doctors would sometimes prescribe 'a course of waters' at one of the Spa towns. King George III was sent to Cheltenham where he drank a pint and a half a day of the unpleasant tasting, purgative water.

A Newport surgeon, Thomas L. Waterworth, discovered a chalybeate spring in 1808, midway between Niton and Blackgang. In 1810 he leased ground from Charles Anderson Pelham, Lord Yarborough, built a reservoir and erected a thatched dispensary, called Sandrock Spring Cottage. The water was used as a remedy for the physical weakness caused by Walcheren fever, brought back by soldiers involved in the disastrous Walcheren Expedition of 1809. The strong mineral content was regarded as successful in treating 'prostration of the nervous energy . . . and many disorders of the female constitution' like menorrhagia. An 1824 guide book talks of "the essential benefit for afflictive cases of stern disease or sluggish debility" and the water's power to remedy "the tremblings."

Water from the spring was analysed by a Dr Marcet who found 41 grains of iron sulphate per pint and 31 grains of alumina. The brown liquid was unpleasant to taste and nauseous, acting as a purgative if taken in large quantities. Dr George Martin in his 1849 treatise *The Undercliff of the Isle of Wight* regarded it as "best exhibited in soda water, commencing with about a dessert-spoonful as a dose three times daily, gradually increased up to an ounce and a half . . . in larger doses its astringent properties interfere with its other effects." A visitor to the spring in 1826 wrote, one "may take a bottle of this precious water on payment of half a crown, or drink a glass, but ten to one it makes you sick, as it tastes like ink."

Gothic stone arch over the spring

The doctor built a shrine over the source of the spring with a gothic stone arch and trefoil window which made it look like a church porch and was supposed to represent a hermit's cell. A Latin hexameter on the wall of the chapel-like building read "Infirmo capiti fluit utilis, utilis alvo" (the water which flows here is useful for those who have a weak head or stomach). The stone grotto has long since collapsed into the sea and the buildings disappeared in the landslip of 1979.

The doctor made a lot of money, the difficulty of access and foul tasting water suited the Victorian belief that the road to health is necessarily arduous and painful! Rock Cottage was built in 1790 and bought by a pair of Newport brewers in 1810 who saw its potential following the discovery of the mineral spring. They turned it into the Sandrock Hotel and enlarged it in 1818. The Duchess of Kent and her daughter, the Princess Victoria visited the hotel in the spring in 1834, the Duchess granting permission for the addition of Royal to the hotel name.

Early success didn't last and hopes that Sandrock would one day rival Cheltenham and Tonbridge Wells were just pie in the sky. Visitors staying at the Royal Sandrock Hotel found the walk to the dispensary difficult and it was largely ignored. By 1860 it had closed but the hotel thrived until engulfed by a fire in 1984.

CHAPTER SEVEN

A POET'S PILLAR

Wilkes' Doric Column

The English radical journalist and politician, John Wilkes, is often credited as the 'discoverer' of Sandown. When he built a cottage and settled down in the Isle of Wight it was on a common called 'Royal Heath,' the site of the present town. Apart from Sandham Cottage, which Wilkes called his 'villakin,' the only other buildings of note were Sandham Fort and the barracks (behind The Heights Sports Centre). There was, as yet, no such place as Sandown.

What Wilkes brought with him to the island was notoriety. He married an heiress with a large estate and lead a life of dissipation and profligacy, especially as a member of the Hellfire Club. When his marriage and the money fizzled out he faced ruin and decided to 'try his chance' in Parliament. In 1757 he was elected MP for Aylesbury. When in 1762 the new king, George III, arranged for his close friend, Lord Bute, to become Prime Minister, Wilkes was his leading critic in the House of Commons. He established a newspaper, the *North Briton*, as a vehicle for attacking Bute which eventually lead to his resignation.

In 1763, John Wilkes was arrested for seditious libel but was released after the Lord Chief Justice ruled that MPs were protected by parliamentary privilege from prosecution for libel. Wilkes continued to attack the government and when Parliament revoked MPs protection Wilkes fled to France and didn't return until 1768.

Wilkes was a friend of the English poet and satirist, Charles Churchill, who worked closely with Wilkes on the *North Briton*. *The Prophecy of Famine*, subtitled *A Scots Pastoral*, was dedicated to Wilkes and first appeared, although in a different form, in his newspaper. It was a violent satire on Lord Bute and Scottish place seekers and Churchill continued to write virulent satires against Wilkes' enemies until October 1764 when he joined his friend in Boulogne. There he was

The Pillar in the garden of Wilke's 'villakin'

attacked by a fever of which he died on 4th November.

Churchill's deathbed will made Wilkes his literary executor with full powers so his papers and his reputation were left entirely in Wilkes' hands. But his friend did little except write half a dozen notes on his poems and contribute to a biography of Churchill.

When Wilkes was burnt out as a political figure, 'the volcano nearly extinct,' he retired to his 'villakin' and spent his time in his study revising "his work" which he intended for posthumous publication under the title *Life and Opinions of John Wilkes*. There he belatedly responded to his friend's death by erecting a Doric column, along the lines of Virgil's tomb, in the grounds of his cottage. A visitor wrote, "In the shrubbery of Wilkes' cottage is a monument shaded by a cypress and a weeping willow tree, raised to Churchill's memory. It is made of oak, painted white, a fluted pillar eight feet high and fourteen inches

in diameter, and in the centre is a tablet with the inscription:-

> Carlo Churchill
>
> Divino Poetae
>
> Amico jucundo
>
> Civi Optime de Patria merito

Translated it read "To the divine poet, the genial friend, the citizen deserving of his country's highest regard." The base of the column was hollow and kept stocked with the finest port in the poet's honour.

Alas the cottage and column are gone though there is a commemorative plaque to Wilkes and his 'villakin' in the road that bears his name. The Rev Venables wrote, in 1860, that the "cottage which first made Sandown famous has been lately swept away by the march of so-called improvement, regardless of the historical interest attaching to the spot."

Edward Thomas bemoaned the loss of the monument saying "there would have been something unpleasantly touching in the sight of the insolent yet pitiful stone... ... set up to the memory of a dead acquaintance in a country garden he had never visited."

CHAPTER EIGHT
PEPPER-POT PENANCE

A Fog Folly

In medieval times islanders living along the 'Back of the Wight' struggled to make a living from fishing and working on the land. A ship wrecked off these treacherous coasts may have been a disaster for shipowner, merchant and sailors, but it was a bonus for the coastal communities. Every parish had its slice of coastline, because 'wreck' was an important source of income:-

> Good ship oak to mend the hearth
> Rich stores that may not sink,
> And, if perchance, she hail from France,
> Good Gascon wine to drink.

Walter de Godeton, Lord of the Manor of Chale, certainly benefited from wreck to the extent that he was prepared to take on the English courts and risk his soul by angering the Pope!

In 1313, the *St Mary of Bayonne* sailed from Gascony with a cargo which included 147 casks of white wine from the Duchy of Aquitaine. She was making for the monastery at Livers in Picardy but was blown off course and came ashore in Chale Bay. It wasn't long before islanders for miles around were gathering on the beach and began pilfering whatever the tide brought in. The shipwrecked crew joined in by selling off the wine, perhaps too afraid of the throng to do otherwise. Fifty-three barrels of wine worth four marks each found their way into Sir Walter's cellars.

Sir Walter claimed they were his by right of wreck but the merchants of Aquitaine who chartered the ship were not easily put off. As subjects of the English Crown they appealed to the courts for justice. De Godeton and three others were summoned to appear at the Southampton courts; three times they ignored the summons but when they eventually appeared they were fined 267 marks with 20 marks damages, a considerable sum in those days. But Sir Walter was rich and he quickly paid off his fines. But that wasn't the end of the matter – it seemed Sir Walter had upset the pope!

Sir Walter's crime reached the ears of Pope Clement V who, perhaps angered at the taking of church property, declared he must be punished.

A Papal Bull was issued threatening excommunication unless due restitution and penance was made. He was told to build a lighthouse on top of St Catherine's Down and with it a chantry where a priest can say prayers for Sir Walter's family and all those who perish at sea. He was to provide an income sufficient to keep it manned and in operation in perpetuity.

Sir Walter did as he was bid and built a lighthouse thirty-five and a half feet high, octangular with a pyramidal roof and a chantry attached to the side. It is claimed that priests prayed and tended the beacon for 212 years. During the reign of Henry VIII, when he ordered the dissolution of the monasteries, the chantry was dismantled. But it was never very effective as a lighthouse for one very good reason. It was built . . .

> On the lonely crown of Catherine's Down
> Where the mists hang chill and damp.

Mist, fog and low cloud were constantly swirling around the down hiding the light from view.

Was it not folly to build a lighthouse where it couldn't be seen? This folly was compounded when in 1785 work started on a second lighthouse close by but this was never finished – because of fog! Around the same time Sir Richard Worsley had the old lighthouse buttressed to preserve it which makes it look like a rocketship ready for take-off. Known as the 'Pepperpot' it is one of the island's most famous landmarks seen for miles around and each year many thousands of visitors trudge up the hill to investigate this curiosity.

CHAPTER NINE

LUCCOMBE CHINE TOWER

A Chasm Conundrum

Compared to Shanklin's luxuriant chasm, the chine at Luccombe is less spectacular, being of smaller dimensions and with less profuse and varied foliage. Shanklin is brash where Luccombe is unassuming, the entrance at the head of the chine appears unannounced in comparison to Shanklin's loud trumpet-blowing. In 1873 a representative from *Punch* magazine complained he "had to pay eighteen pence to see this Shanklin toy." Two years later, another visitor, J. Redding Ware, wrote that "for those who love the natural without the intrusion of the artificial, Luccombe Chine is the most delightful in the Isle."

The residences in and around the chine mirrored the divisions of Victorian society. Upstairs, at the head of the chine, was a charming cottage ornee, enveloped in a profusion of creepers and surrounded by fine oaks. A little to the west was Rosecliff, a genteel residence owned by the Freres and built of warm tinted stone procured nearby. Downstairs, on a terrace of slumped cliff, were a number of labourer's cottages. On the north side of the chine, lived Pound Hammer Kingswell and his wife. On the other side lived the Kemps, Buttons, Crosses and Tom Hardy and there was room for a small chapel. These five families earnt a precarious living from fishing and potting, and a little farm work on nearby estates. Occasionally, an east wind, known as a 'luccomber,' would force a ship onto the rocks, providing an unexpected harvest of goods and materials, especially if the ship broke up.

It was, nevertheless, a community. Miss Frere would play the organ at chapel (or sometimes Miss Jolliffe from Luccombe Farm). Pound Hammer, a keen tobacco chewer, had a seat reserved for him just inside the door of the chapel so he could spit outside. If it wasn't

Brannon engraving of Luccombe Chine circa 1840

religion that kept 'upstairs' and 'downstairs' together perhaps it was the shared hazards of smuggling. The Kingswells were all involved, Charlie Kingswell most of all. There were underground cellars in their cottages, the caves in the nearby cliffs could hide a hundred tubs, and the rocky ledges, well known to the fishermen, were ideal spots to sink tubs while waiting for things to cool off. Perhaps 'upstairs' provided the finance, while 'downstairs' did the donkey work? Farmer Jolliffe was certainly suspected by the customs officers.

A landslip in 1910 put an end to Luccombe's fishing community and the families were moved to Shanklin. Rosecliff succumbed to sudsidence in 1938; perhaps it was this landslip that put an end to the circular stone tower that was perched on the western edge of the chine. Certainly, it was in the 1940's that Sir Arthur Fleming, who then owned Luccombe Chine House (the old cottage ornee enlarged), had the present tower built to the original design. The tower was made of battered stone, so it flared at the base, with a one storey crenellated parapet with flagpole, a lancet window and arch doorway. The original tower was further west and survives in a George Brannon engraving of 1834; this places its construction in the early part of the century when gothic revival architecture was in vogue. Today, as you descend the footpath that winds down the chine to the shore, it peeps at you through the trees, on the very edge of the precipice, a union flag gaily flapping in the breeze.

As to its purpose, if indeed there was one, we may never know. Some believe it to be a Customs and Excise watchtower, yet the smuggling community were far too wily to be caught while that was manned. Maybe it was the other way round? Was it a smuggler's lookout where they could watch for the boat's arrival; yet why such a fancy tower? This mimic tower, as Brannon calls it, is a fanciful creation, a capricious indulgence, a fantasy, fairytale castle where, perhaps, young ladies growing up at Rosecliff or Chine House could dream of their sailor lovers returning from over the sea. Or perhaps it was simply a retreat where one could retire to and enjoy the view through the lush ravine and out to the ever-changing sea. If ever there was a folly in its purest sense, then this is it, for its purpose seems to be "to just be there!"

Luccombe Chine Tower today

CHAPTER TEN

OLD NEEDLES LIGHTHOUSE

Another Fog Folly

On a visit to the Isle of Wight in 1811, geologist Thomas Webster wrote of the Needles: "Scarcely a winter passes without one or more shipwrecks in this place; many vessels choosing to risk this shorter passage to and from Portsmouth, instead of going round by St Helens. Two lighthouses are erected at Hurst Castle, to direct the pilots to clear the Needles; but in hazy weather fatal mistakes are too frequent."

One man who was well aware of the dangers of the Needles channel was mapmaker and surveyor Grenville Collins, who was appointed by Charles II to survey the coasts of Britain. In 1693 he published a chart of the Isle of Wight with accompanying 'Directions.' He noted that the 'indraught' at the Needles "hath hauld many ships into Freshwater Bay." His advice was "mind the lead; the neglect of which hath been the loss of many ships. Keep a five-and-twenty and thirty fathom water, and you need not fear the indraught of Wight."

Among the dangers to beware of were strong eddies and currents, shallow water over the Shingles Bank and the rocks of the Needles themselves. One of the ships to fall foul of these perils was *HMS*

Assurance, a 40-gun warship, lost at the Needles in 1753.She was bound from Lisbon with the retiring governor of Jamaica and his wife aboard. All were saved. In 1765 the *Apthorp*, sailing from Dieppe to Topsam in ballast, was stranded in Scratchell's Bay. The *Philicay Racket*, a Carolina rice ship, foundered at the Needles in 1774 with the loss of its cargo and in 1781 the 300-ton *Roberts* was lost.

Because of these hazards, a custom of pilotage grew up and Yarmouth, the nearest haven to the Needles, was the base for half a dozen pilots licensed by Trinity House. The pilots often faced great danger, sailing their small cutters out to meet the big ships, and were hardy, skilled men and well rewarded. But this was clearly not enough for in 1781 a group of merchants and shipowners petitioned Trinity House (which was responsible for 'beaconage, bouyage and ballastage') for a more permanent navigation aid.

So, in 1785, Trinity House began construction of three new lighthouses – at Hurst Castle, the Needles and St Catherine's Down, all of which were to prove white elephants, or follies. The one at St Catherine's, so close to the old medieval one, was never completed when it was realised it would be dogged by the same problem as the old one – fog. The one at Hurst Castle was replaced in 1811 following the loss of *HMS Pommone*. The Needles lighthouse lasted somewhat longer, being replaced in 1859, though it proved largely ineffectual, too often shrouded in fog.

The lighthouse was a squat, truncated cone-shaped building erected 474 feet above sea level on a summit known as St Christophers. It began operation on 29 September 1786, its light powered by ten argand lamps and the same number of plated reflectors, consuming 700 gallons of fish oil a year (an argand lamp was an oil lamp invented by Swiss scientist Aimee Argand which had a steady smokeless flame that was to revolutionise lighthouse illumination). It took the full force of the prevailing wind; in hard-blowing weather "very large flints and fragments of chalk are blown from the cliffs so as to endanger the windows of the lighthouse, and for many days in succession it is scarcely possible to open the door. In summer the reflectors had to be curtained to prevent the sunshine being focused and magnified so as to set fire to the surrounding grass!

The losses continued. The *Countess Hoberton* foundered in 1793, the navy lost the frigate *HMS Guernsey Lily* in the Needles channel in 1799, and the *Pilgrim* went down in 1811. That same year saw *HMS Pommone* sunk after impaling herself on Goose Rock, that perilous outcrop of the Needles. The 38-gun, 1,076 ton warship was just six years old with a crew of 284 when she went down under identical circumstances to *Assurance.*

Tragedy of a more sinister nature befell the lighthouse in November 1832 when the lighthouse keeper, Thomas Colereine, who lived in the adjoining buildings with his wife and seven children, fell to his death from Highdown Cliff into the sea amidst rumours that he was murdered by smugglers. His wife kept the light burning for another year. In the early nineteenth century the lighthouse was a popular stop for the increasing numbers of visitors.

The old lighthouse, so often buried in mist and low cloud, had to await the ambitious plan of the architect James Walker for its

Site of Old Needles Lighthouse

replacement, for it needed to be at sea level. Walker's plan was to dynamite the outermost sea stack to create a platform on which to construct a granite tower with a stepped base. The new lighthouse was finished in 1859 and the old one fell into disuse and was soon dismantled. Considering the experience with other lighthouses built on heights prone to fog was it folly to build it on the promontory nearly 500 feet above the sea? For though 'serviceable,' wrecks continued with monotonous regularity. Or was it the best that could be achieved at the time?

CHAPTER ELEVEN
THE FOLLY INN
A folly in name only

The Medina estuary is tidal all the way to Newport which, being at the navigable limit of the river, and centrally placed, flourished as the island's principal market town. In the eighteenth century grain was the most important product; the island was considered "the granary of the western counties" and the chief resource of the government contracts to supply the navy and, towards the end of the century, the armies in America and the West Indies, with wheat, malt, flour and biscuit. There were eight or nine mills around Newport, including one on either side of the Medina. There would have been a steady traffic of sailing barges laden with flour for export or bringing coal and manufactures to fill the warehouses built beside the busy Town Quay.

There was once a sloop named *La Folie,* which was moored at a bend in the river opposite a place called Werrar, and it served refreshments to the bargemasters sailing up to Newport with their cargoes. On low water spring tides this part of the river almost dries out so barges unable to make it upriver would wait in what is now called Folly Reach for the next tide; in the meantime, bargemasters could take advantage of the refreshments on offer aboard *La Folie.* One day, following a storm and an exceptionally high spring tide, she came adrift from her moorings and was left high and dry on the riverbank. Despite the efforts of the captain she could not be floated off. So the captain settled down there and built around the stranded hulk and gradually *La Folie* became the Folly Inn.

The first written mention of the Folly is in 1725 and an Admiralty chart of 1783 depicts the Folly like Noah's Ark, so still recognisably a boat at that time. By the early nineteenth century *The Folly* belonged to Captain Thomas Burnett who owned several trading craft and a fleet of oyster vessels and employed somebody to run the Inn, now permanently grounded. An Admiralty chart of 1853 describes the Inn as the Folly Halfway House, a convenient watering hole indeed. While renovating the inn during 1964, workmen discovered some of the ship's old ribs, a section of which is visible behind a glass panel in the floor for all to see.

Folly Inn around 1910

Bob Savage, the inn's popular landlord from around 1905 to the mid-30s, organised the first Folly Regatta on 20 September 1913 for which it has since become famous. The programme included boat races of all kinds and land amusements which included walking the greasy pole, tug-of-war (married ladies versus single) and an Eating Treacle Bun Race. There was also dancing on the green with music supplied by the band of Princess Beatrice's Isle of Wight Rifles. The old country game of Ring the Bull was played on an old pear tree outside the inn with a rope and an iron ring.

The First World War interrupted what was intended as an annual regatta until it was revived in the 1930s with the eccentric Uffa Fox as Pesident of the Organising Committee. A popular event was the beer barrel race; a tub of beer was tied to a pile and teams in rowing boats competed to bring it ashore.

Since the 1960s the Folly Inn has encouraged the yachting and dinghy sailing fraternity by laying down moorings. In the summer season there is much jostling for visitor's berths for the Folly is a popular stopover for yachtsmen. With a track record of over 200 years providing refreshments to users of the Medina River, the Folly is, in truth, anything but a folly!

CHAPTER TWELVE

BAD START FOR SMART ART

The Land Sea Light Cone at St Mary's Hospital

When the Koan, which stands at the entrance to St Mary's Hospital, was commissioned by Healing Arts, in 1996, nobody anticipated the long-running rumpus it would cause; rather than acting as a healing aid, the koan has raised temperatures and blood pressures and sent many islanders into apoplectic fits of letter-writing. It is a folly in two senses; not only is it an absurd waste of money, but it serves no useful purpose. It creates anger and wrath, quite the opposite intention to that of its creator.

This wasn't the first koan Liliane Lijn had designed and built. Twenty years ago the American-born artist built a smaller koan for the Mead Gallery at Warwick University. Guy Eades, administrator for Healing Arts at St Mary's, said, "The Warwick Koan was an early example of the artist's work and has suffered from lack of maintenance and that is no fault of the design."

However, Sarah Shaigoky, curator of the Mead Gallery, claimed, "There were certain design flaws identified by structural engineers who looked at our koan, which would probably be well-suited to the

Arizona Desert but not to Plymouth where ours used to be. I just hope the St Mary's Koan is not going to be sited where the air is salty!"

The Land Sea Light Koan, to give it the full title, is a 26ft high cone painted in rainbow coloured bands which swirl around as sections of the Koan revolve and light up. Ms Lijn said, "The imagery of it is inspired by the island's geology, with its famous coloured rock and sand strata together with the navigation bouys and beacons of the inshore waters and the Solent." She was convinced of its therapeutic value claiming

Photo courtesy of the Isle of Wight County Press

the koan spoke of change and renewal, transforming itself with the changing light of day and night throughout the seasons.

But two months after it was officially handed over to the health authority, in April 1997, the koan was not revolving nor was it lighting up. The koan, which cost £55,000 to build and install, has provoked more letters to the County Press than any other topic in recent years. Critics argue that the money would have been better spent on patient care and that maintenance and running costs would be a constant drain on resources.

Leading opposition to the koan was Peter Corby, a businessman from Cowes, who organised a 4,000 signature petition to have the koan removed. Local people were "angry, aggravated and insulted" by the structure which "should be returned under the Sale of Goods Act." Mr Corby "was sure they could sell it to Robin Hill or Butlins where it will look very nice."

Despite threats to the artist to get the koan working as intended the problems continued with the koan illuminated and revolving only sporadically. It was rapidly becoming a modern day folly and a millstone round the neck of the IW Healthcare Trust. Despite assurances that none of the £55,000 came from patient care funds but was largely funded by the Lottery, the overwhelming feeling of islanders was that this was a waste of money.

The IW Healthcare Trust found themselves in a 'no win situation' with the koan. If they ordered its removal the Trust would be forced to pay back a £31,000 Arts Council National Lottery grant out of health service funds. They could also face litigation from the artist. And so for the last ten years the koan has stood sentinel outside the entrance to St Mary's Hospital, neither revolving nor illuminated, a monument to good intentions gone wrong.

CHAPTER THIRTEEN
A TALE OF TWO TABLETS

Hoy's Monument

On 6 June 1814 Tsar Alexander I of Russia disembarked at Dover. He was on a triumphal journey through Europe in the wake of the victory over Napoleon. In London he was met by euphoric crowds and was mobbed wherever he went. The mood was one of celebration, not just over the visit of the Tsar, but over the wider peace in Europe embodied in the just-signed Treaty of Paris.

While in London the Tsar was taken to places of interest by British royalty. He went to the theatre, the Ascot races and watched a military review in Hyde Park. There were, of course, the usual round of splendid dinners held in his honour; the dinner at the Guildhall was the highlight of his visit and the guest list would surely have included Michael Hoy as an ex-Sheriff of London and prominent Russian trader. When the royal party went to Portsmouth for two days to review the fleet, Michael Hoy would doubtless have been there to see his hero. It was in this atmosphere of jubilation that Michael commissioned the Niton stonemason, Andrew Morris, to build an Alexandrian pillar on land he owned.

Perched on top of the long ridge of St Catherine's Down, Hoy's monument is one of the island's outstanding landmarks, and can be seen for miles around. It is an imposing edifice, a stone pillar seventy-two feet high (nearly 24 metres) topped with a finial ball. A plaque on the base reads:-

"In commemoration of the visit of His Majesty Tsar Alexander I, Emperor of all the Russias, to Great Britain in 1814. In remembrance of many happy years residence in his dominions this pillar was erected by Michael Hoy."

From afar it looks like a solitary candle on a cake, yet this is no whimsical decoration; this is the physical manifestation of one man's gratitude to a king and country that was his making in the world. Russia made Michael Hoy a wealthy man.

Michael was born in 1758 into a trading family; his father, Richard, was a merchant in Picadilly and his mother, Margaret, ran a honey warehouse. As a young man of 24 Hoy was living in St Petersburg and operating, with a partner, a retail shop, known simply as the English shop, selling luxury goods from the west to the Russian aristocracy. Four years later, in 1786, he was admitted to the Russia Company which allowed him into the lucrative import/export trade.

The Russia Company was founded in Tudor times to trade with Russia selling western manufactured goods, particularly cloth and armaments, in exchange for her raw materials. In 1778 nearly 900 ships made their way down the Baltic in the warmer summer months with cargoes of iron ore, timber, flax and furs. In 1782 there were up to five hundred Britons living and working in Russia. Back in England Hoy set up business in the City of London, trading as a Russia merchant and became well known amongst the society of public officials, financiers and bankers. In 1792 he became a Yeoman of the Worshipful Company of Ironmongers and in 1798 a Freeman of the City of London for which honour he paid a princely sum of forty six shillings and eight pence. For the year 1812/13 he was Sheriff of London, perhaps the highlight of his career.

With his wealth Hoy bought extensive estates on the island including the manors of Chale and Walpen, Gotten and Dolcoppice Farm; by 1825 he owned some 1,700 acres in the south of the island around St Catherine's Down. He invested in progressive local projects and was among those who started The Ryde Pier Company. He had shares in two cross-Solent steam packets and became a Highway Commissioner for Whitwell. He was known for his liberality and bounty, as a patron of the arts and subscriber to various local projects.

Under the brow at the northern end of St Catherine's Down lies Medina Hermitage which Brannon describes as having a "rich prospect of the whole of the county" and the house's greatest feature "a large and elegant verandah." Hoy bought the house around 1809 and probably had it rebuilt and renamed "The Hermitage" possibly after the Hermitage Museum in St Petersburg. In the middle of the square onto which the Hermitage Museum faced was a tall pillar set on a square base - the inspiration behind the monument he was to build just a few years later.

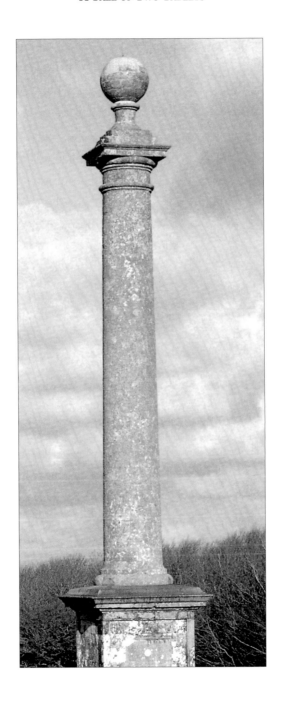

Michael Hoy was grateful to Russia not only for his personal betterment but also for the crucial role she played in the alliance against Napoleon. Forty years on, France is now an ally and Russia, the 'Great Bear,' the enemy. As Turkey, the 'Sick Man of Europe,' disintegrated Britain feared Russian encroachment in central Europe could threaten British interests, especially India. So Britain drifted into a war in the Crimea.

William Henry Dawes, nephew of the notorious Sophie Dawes, was now in possession of the Hermitage. Sophie made a fortune as mistress to the Duc de Bourbon and looked after her relatives. Doubtless it was Sophie that bought him the Hermitage as well as the commission in the 43rd Regiment of Foot. He spent eight years in the Army, then retired from the service and settled on the island.

When war broke out there was much animosity towards the Russians and Dawes, as an ex-soldier, would have felt an even keener enmity towards them. How the monument erected by Michael Hoy must have rankled; so he added his own tablet. The inscription read:-

> "This tablet was erected by William Henry Dawes late Lieutenant of H.M. 22 Reg. in honour of those brave men of the allied armies who fell on the Alma at Inkerman and at the siege of Sevastopol. AD 1857."

So visitors drawn by curiosity to this island landmark are faced with two contradictory sentiments. Though not strictly a folly in the pure sense, nevertheless its prominence, curiosity value and clash of opinions expressed on the tablets allow its inclusion.

CHAPTER FOURTEEN
APPLEY TOWER

A fantasy, fairytale folly

Appley Watchtower bears the motto "Vouloir et Pouvoir" – the Will and the Power – a fitting aphorism for Sir William Hutt who built it. Britain relied on families like the Hutts to furnish her with the warriors and administrators she required to keep the machinery of Empire moving. The Hutts provided a number of distinguished members of Britain's political and military hierarchy who, for a time, lived – and died – at Appley, near Ryde.

Appley House was built by the notorious smuggler, David Boyce, from the profits of his trade. For a while it belonged to the Hutts who also owned the neighbouring estate of Appley Towers. John Hutt was a captain in the navy, in command of the brig Antigua on the Jamaica station, when she was seized and burnt. Hutt and his crew were captured but after an exchange of prisoners Hutt returned to England and was tried, but acquitted, of the loss of his ship. In 1793 he was appointed to command the Queen (98 guns) as flag captain to Rear Admiral Alan Gardner, whom he had known on the Jamaica station, and was involved in the unsuccessful attempt to retake Martinique. On 29 May 1794 he lost a leg in a preliminary engagement to the famous battle known as the 'Glorious First of June' and died on the last day of the month.

Appley Tower was also the seat of Sir William Hutt, John Hutt's nephew. Born in 1801 in Lambeth, William was educated privately at Ryde and went on to gain a degree at Cambridge. In 1831 he married Mary, dowager countess of Strathmore and lived at Streatlam Castle in Durham. The following year he entered Parliament as MP for Hull, then from 1841 to 1874 he represented Gateshead. His wife died in

1860 leaving him mining properties with an income £18,000 per annum. A year later Sir William married a daughter of Sir James Francis Stanhope. His career peaked when he was made Paymaster General and VicePresident of the Board of Trade in 1860. Five years later he was made a Knight Commander of the Order of the Bath and became Sir William Hutt.

William Hutt

William's brother George was a distinguished officer in the old Indian artillery and served in the Scinde and Afghan campaigns. He commanded artillery in the Persian War of 1857 and rendered valuable aid to Sir Bartle Frere in Scinde during the mutiny. On retirement from the army the old soldier took a more mundane position, as Registrar and Secretary to the Commissioners of Chelsea Hospital, a position he held until 1886. That same year George received the KCB and died at Appley Towers three years later.

William was greatly interested in colonial affairs at a time when Britain was looking to colonisation as a means of relieving the distress and 'overpopulation' as a result of economic depression. He was a commissioner for the foundation of South Australia; the Hutt River in the province's Clare Valley was named after him and another brother John was to become Western Australia's second governor.

But it was New Zealand which was his real interest. From 1837 he was a member of the New Zealand Association, a member of the select committee on New Zealand in 1840 and a founder member of the New Zealand Company of which he was later a director and chairman. The principal agent for the company was to be William Wakefield, a colonel in the Portugese Army, brother of Edward Gibbon Wakefield who expounded new colonisation schemes in his Letter from Sydney, published in 1829.

Following a farewell speech given by William Hutt, William Wakefield set sail aboard the Tory with instructions to acquire land from the Maoris and prepare an area for settlement. The Tory arrived in what is now Wellington harbour on September 20 1839 and began to buy up land around the Heretaunga river valley, which was renamed the Hutt river in honour of William Hutt. By 8 November he had bought up large areas either side of the Cook Strait; in all he bought 20 million acres in exchange for muskets, umbrellas and jews' harps. The first settlers arrived the following year and from the very beginning there were disputes over land ownership which wrangled on for thirty years and even persist today. Today the cities of Lower Hutt and Upper Hutt are thriving suburbs of Wellington.

William retired to the Isle of Wight to live out his days at Appley. What motivated Sir William to build such an oddity as the fairytale tower and what purpose, if any, did it serve? Today it sells sea-shell souvenirs and trinkets to tourists and possibly acted as a look-out post for enemy aircraft during the Second World War. We know it served as a tea-rooms selling teas to Victorian matrons pushing their charges along the esplanade, so was it built to keep an old man, who has lead a busy life, occupied? It looks like a fantasy castle from a children's fairytale, but William had no children from either marriage. Perhaps it was his brother George's children that inspired him to build it. Or was the island's taste in architecture featuring castellated turrets the inspiration? Was it an indulgent watchtower built to view the waters of Spithead busy with naval warships, commercial shipping and private yachts. The truth doesn't really matter for it is a delight to the eye, a true eyecatcher indeed! When William Hutt died in 1882 he left his brother George all his landed property which included this distinctive landmark.

CHAPTER FIFTEEN
THE TEMPLE IN THE TREES

Swainston's Eyecatcher

"They have just passed the entrance-gates of Swaynestone – lonely gates, unfurnished with a lodge – and the waggon stops with interrupted music at some smaller gates on the other side of the road, where the upland still rises, not in bare down, but in rich meadow, to a hanging wood, out of which peeps dimly in the dusk a small white structure, built with a colonnade supporting an architrave, to imitate a Greek temple – Alma's home."

Alma, heroine of Maxwell Gray's popular novel *The Silence of Dean Maitland*, lived in the Temple at Swainston that stares out from the trees on the south side of the Calbourne Road. This is probably the "Temple Arch" that was commissioned in the late eighteenth century around the same time that the present House at Swainston was built. It was meant as a summerhouse though facing north, towards the house, it was exposed to the north wind. It is aptly called the "Temple of Boreas," Greek god of the north wind.

Swainston Manor was built on the site of the summer palace of the Bishops of Winchester. It was Sir John Barrington who rebuilt the house in around 1750 using the old foundations and parts of the older building. The Barringtons owned Swainston for nearly 300 years though Sir John, the seventh baronet, was the first to make it his permanent home. He represented Newtown in Parliament on and off for nearly 50 years.

The temple is not really a temple at all but a façade, a portico leading nowhere, an eyecatcher meant to be seen from the main house, an embellishment to the view looking south. Built against a backdrop of trees the columns of the false Greek temple stand out amidst the greenery.

It was in such surroundings that a warm and beautiful friendship grew between Tennyson and Sir John Simeon whose father acquired

Swainston through marriage. It was John who badgered Tennyson into reviving work on *Maud,* the dramatic poem that was to make him comfortable financially for the rest of his life. Tennyson, grief-stricken at Sir John's death in 1870, wrote the sad little poem *In the garden at Swainston* as a tribute to Sir John whom he called the Prince of Courtesy.

The temple still stares out from the greenery and is protected as a listed building. It was once offered for sale in the hope that some rich romantic with a classical bent may be tempted with such a curious oddment. It has acquired its place on the Ordnance Survey map as simply the Temple in a strip of green called the Temple Plantation. But the car-bound tourist of today probably wouldn't notice it so it is no longer the eyecatcher it once was.

CHAPTER SIXTEEN
ST JOHNS, RYDE

A Gothic Folly

St Johns House was built for Colonel William Amherst in 1769 and takes its name from St Johns in Newfoundland where the Colonel had been Governor. The Amhersts were pillars of the Empire with a colourful history. William had two brothers – John, an admiral in the navy and Jeffrey, Commander-in-Chief of operations in British North America who, after the fall of Montreal in 1760, was appointed Governor-General. In 1781 the house passed to William's son, William Pitt Amherst, a Governor-General of British India, who leased it out. In 1796 it was bought by Edward Simeon of London who took a great interest in the estate.

A year earlier Humphry Repton had published his *Sketches and Hints on Landscape Gardening* and it was Repton who was employed to lay out the grounds. Repton's way was to prepare a 'Red Book' for his clients showing how their grounds could be improved but the 'Red Book' for St Johns has been lost.

Repton turned surrounding fields into parkland and laid out walks in the wood. A new entrance with two thatched lodges was built and there was The Marina, an ornamental building used for bathing and sea watching. None of these structures survive. Cooke's engraving of 1808, in his *New Pictures of the Isle of Wight*, shows The Marina, which overlooks the wooded shore, as a substantial building. Described as "a pretty Gothic or Moorish castle," it must have been used for more than just bathing and viewing the sea; "a promenade on Sunday

evening through these walks was enlivened by a band of music from The Marina, affording an exhilarating scene of innocent recreation." It was demolished sometime in the nineteenth century.

Edward Simeon died in 1812 and the estate passed to his nephew, Richard Godin Simeon who enlarged it to over 300 acres. On 8 April 1813 he married Louisa Edith Barrington, daughter of Sir Fitzwilliam Barrington of Swainston. When Sir Fitzwilliam died he inherited the estate, via his wife. When he died in 1854 his son, John Simeon, took over both estates.

In 1865 St John's was broken up, the house being sold with just 16 acres of grounds. Six years later it was bought by John Peter Gassiot, a wine merchant, magistrate and distinguished amateur scientist. Gassiot was friendly with Michael Faraday and worked with him on research into electricity. He was elected to the Royal Society in 1840 and in 1863 won the Society's Royal (gold) Medal in recognition of his work on voltaic electricity. He engaged William Page, a respected landscape gardener from Southampton, to redesign the grounds. Page had been responsible for laying out the grounds of Steephill Castle and his work there attracted praise from the famous professional gardener, Joseph Paxton.

Some features of Page's work have survived within the grounds of the house which is now the home of Bishop Lovett Middle School. In particular there are the remains of a seven-sided mock Gothic folly now almost hidden by the trees that crowd around it and the ivy climbing its walls. Each side had a tall lancet arch window so they could be seen from any direction within the ground and from the house. Its function is to draw the eye, decorate and embellish the grounds, to just "be there."

SUGGESTED WALKS

Walk 1

This walk enjoys fine panoramic views across the 'Back of the Wight' as well as encompassing visits to three of the monuments mentioned in the text – the original St Catherine's Lighthouse and its unfinished replacement and Hoy's Monument.

PARKING: Blackgang Viewpoint Car Park on the A3055 between Niton and Blackgang Chine Theme Park.

ROUTE: Cross the road opposite the car park entrance to the stile. Once over follow the footpath which climbs steadily to the top of the hill. The unfinished stone tower of 1785 lies over the fence but is not worth closer inspection.

To reach Hoy's Monument follow the fenceline northwards down a steep, pitted hillside and head for the wooden gate leading onto a long spur of downland. The monument is visible at the northern end.

Walk 2

Although Cook's Castle no longer exists a stone plinth marks the site and is worth a visit to appreciate its location.

PARKING: Turn left off the main road opposite the Worsley Inn. There is a small car parking area and plenty of kerbside parking.

ROUTE: Walk up Station Road passed the school and the cemetery and, just past Castle Lane, take footpath V30 off to the right and follow to the stone plinth. Return the same way.

To visit the Worsley monument it is worth combining with a visit to Appuldurcombe House during summer opening times.

PARKING: Appuldurcombe House (follow signs from the main road).

ROUTE: From the car park take footpath GL47 to the Freemantle Gate, the imposing arched stone gateway that marks the entrance to the estate. Turn left immediately through the gate onto bridleway GL49. At the top of the rise turn left, over the stone wall, onto footpath GL63 and follow to the obelisk.

Walk 3

A beautiful downland walk with fabulous views to the sea, it is a walk the Bull sisters would have made. Although Northcourt itself is not open to the public it is possible to visit sites mentioned in the text using public footpaths.

PARKING: there is an unmade parking area on the east side of Shorwell Shute next to the quarry.

ROUTE: take the path on the same side of the road that leads to the Alpine Bridge. Cross over and turn right to investigate the Dell, a wooded area which was the site of the mausoleum but there is very little left to see. Otherwise turn left and drop down to the driveway and follow it to the west side of the walled garden and orchard where the path climbs up to a wood by the side of the wall. Turn right through the wood and on leaving it climb up to the ridge on your left. Follow the ridgetop due west, past a dogleg in the path till it begins to merge with the parallel ridge to your right. At a junction next to a grassy old chalk pit there is a small knoll to the south which was the site of the Thimble Cairn. Return the same way.

Walk 4

Great views of the coast against the backdrop of the craggy Undercliff. The coastal footpath passes by Lisle Combe, family home of the poet Alfred Noyes, and once called St Lawrence Cottage (where Sir Richard's mother, Elizabeth, lived) and which adjoined Sea Cottage. The path also passes Old Park, Spindler's home but turns inland before Binnel Bay. It is possible, however, to explore the beach at low water.

PARKING: Use the Car Park at the Botanical Gardens, a mile west of Ventnor on the A3055.

ROUTE: Make your way onto the coastal footpath and follow it west as far as a line of terraced coastguard cottages at Woody Bay where it turns inland. It is possible to get on to the beach at Woody Bay if you wish to continue along the coast. Otherwise, once on the main road, Undercliff Drive (A3055), you can walk up Spindlers Road then turn left at the junction and climb the steps to the clifftop. Walk back along the top until opposite Ventnor Rugby Club you take footpath V73 back to Undercliff Drive.

The **Temple** at Swainston can be seen from the Calbourne Road but there is no public access.

Appley Tower may be visited by walking along the promenade from Ryde Boating Lake towards Puckpool through Appley Park.

The site of **Wilkes'** villakin is marked by a Blue Plaque in Wilkes Road just off the High Street in Sandown though the exact site of his cottage is in doubt.

Old Needles Battery is a National Trust property and **Fort Victoria** a tourist attraction, both open to the public. **Sandown 'granite' Fort** is now the Isle of Wight Zoo. You can drive to the top of Culver Down to see **Bembridge Fort**, but it is not open to the public. **St Helens Sea Fort** can be seen from the shore but there is an annual walk to the fort in August during exceptionally low spring tides.

Luccombe Chine Tower can be seen by taking the steps down through the chine to the beach. To reach the chine you can walk through the Landslip from either Shanklin end or Bonchurch.

The site of the **Shakespeare Memorial** lies along the old Niton Road accessible from Blackgang Chine main car park. As the houses disappear into the tumbled landscape follow the dirt track till you come to a stretch of road again. Look out for the stone scallop where the spring water used to come out and the memorial used to stand on the nearby knoll.

The **Folly Inn** lies at the end of Folly Road off the A3021 Whippingham Road to East Cowes or you can walk alongside the river Medina from the quay at Newport.

St John's gothic folly can be viewed from a footpath. Follow the A3055 main road into Ryde from Sandown past the roundabout at Appley then, halfway down East Hill Road turn right into Ampthill Road. At the end of the road footpath R100 climbs to the right and passes the folly visible through the trees.

The **Koan** can be seen outside the main entrance to St Mary's Hospital.

ACKNOWLEDGEMENTS

County Library Service (esp Lord Louis Reference section and local collection at Somerton), IW County Press, Sarah Burdett, Jeff Brett, Roy Morgan, Mary Case, Bishop Lovett Middle School, Ventnor Heritage Centre.

GRID REFERENCES TO SOME SITES MENTIONED

The Temple, Swainston	440873
Shakespeare Memorial, Blackgang	491762
Miss Bull's Folly, Limerstone	437835
Appley Tower, Ryde	608923
The Koan, Newport	494903
Folly Inn, Whippingham	509929
Worsley Obelisk, Wroxall	537803
Cook's Castle, Wroxall	556804
Hoy's Monument, Niton	495788
Pepperpot, Niton	493775
Sir Richard's Cove (Battery Bay), Undercliff	539764

It is not possible to be specific with Spindler's Folly which lies scattered on the shore between Binnel Bay and Woody Bay. The Sandrock Spring is difficult to locate and is no longer there.

FURTHER READING

Seven Pieces of Eight, Roy Morgan, Sublime Publications, 1970.

The Book of Whippingham, Sarah Burdett, Halsgrove, 2006.

Historic Parks and Gardens of the Isle of Wight, Vicky Basford, I.W.C.C., 1989.

The Island from Within - An Anthology, Patricia Sibley,

Guide to the Isle of Wight, Rev Edmund Venables, Stanford, 1860.

Michael Hoy - The Man and the Monument, Dorothy Wright, Fernlea Publications, 1992.

Wight - Biography of an Island, Paul Hyland, Dovecote Press,

The Isle of Wight - An Illustrated History, Jack and Johanna Jones, Dovecote Press, 1987.

Isle of Wight Curiosities, Jack Jones, Dovecote Press,

Houses by the Sea - Buildings of the Undercliff, 1830-1890, Alan Champion and Jill Wearing, 2000.

Palmerston Forts Society, Fort Nelson, Portsdown Hill Road, Fareham, Hants, PO17 6AN. www.argonet.co.uk/education/dmoore/index.htm

The Portsmouth Papers, 3, 'Palmerston's Folly,' Portsmouth City Council, 1967